FIRST EXPERIENCES

MEL'S MOVING DAY

TOYS

CLOTHES

KITCHEN

GRASSHOPPER

by Alyssa Krekelberg
illustrated by Daniela Massironi

Tools for Parents & Teachers

Grasshopper Books enhance imagination and introduce the earliest readers to fiction with fun storylines and illustrations. The easy-to-read text supports early reading experiences with repetitive sentence patterns and sight words.

Before Reading

- Look at the cover illustration. What do readers see? What do they think the book will be about?
- Look at the picture glossary together. Sound out the words. Ask readers to identify the first letter of each vocabulary word.

Read the Book

- "Walk" through the book, reading to or along with the reader. Point to the illustrations as you read.

After Reading

- Review the picture glossary again. Ask readers to locate the words in the text.
- Ask the reader: How did Mel feel at the start of the book? How did she feel at the end? How do you know?

Grasshopper Books are published by Jump!
5357 Penn Avenue South
Minneapolis, MN 55419
www.jumplibrary.com

Library of Congress Cataloging-in-Publication Data

Names: Krekelberg, Alyssa, author.
Massironi, Daniela, illustrator.
Title: Mel's moving day / by Alyssa Krekelberg;
illustrated by Daniela Massironi.
Description: Minneapolis, MN: Jump!, Inc., 2025.
Series: First experiences
Audience: Ages 3–6
Identifiers: LCCN 2023046367 (print)
LCCN 2023046368 (ebook)
ISBN 9798892130530 (hardcover)
ISBN 9798892130547 (paperback)
ISBN 9798892130554 (ebook)
Subjects: LCSH: Moving, Household—Juvenile fiction.
Readers (Primary) | LCGFT: Readers (Publications).
Classification: LCC PE1119.2 .K746 2025 (print)
LCC PE1119.2 (ebook)
DDC 428.6/2—dc23/eng/20231017
LC record available at https://lccn.loc.gov/2023046367
LC ebook record available at
https://lccn.loc.gov/2023046368

Editor: Jenna Gleisner
Direction and Layout: Molly Ballanger
Illustrator: Daniela Massironi

Printed in the United States of America at
Corporate Graphics in North Mankato, Minnesota.

Table of Contents

A Big Change

We are moving to a new house today.

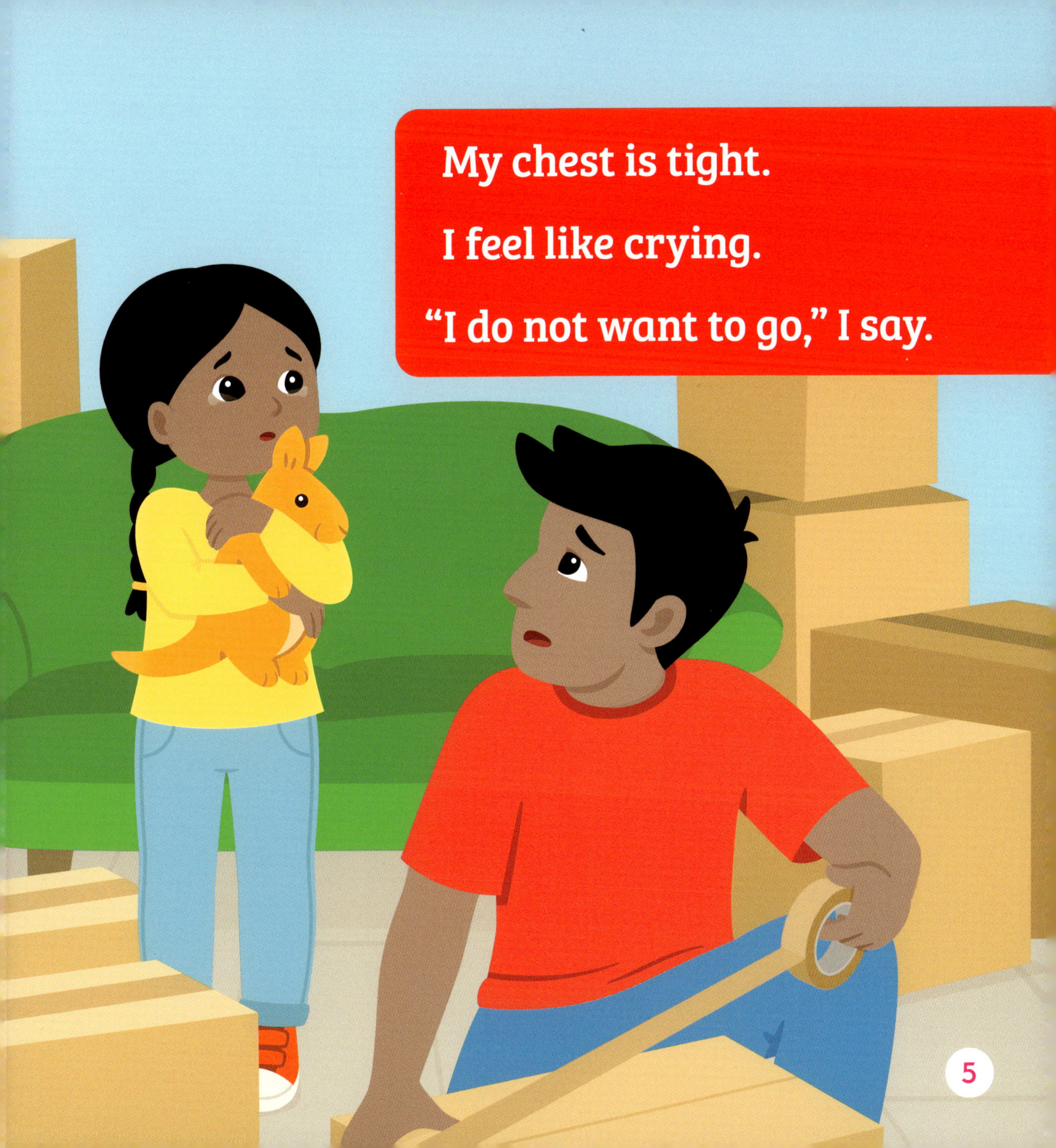

My chest is tight.

I feel like crying.

"I do not want to go," I say.

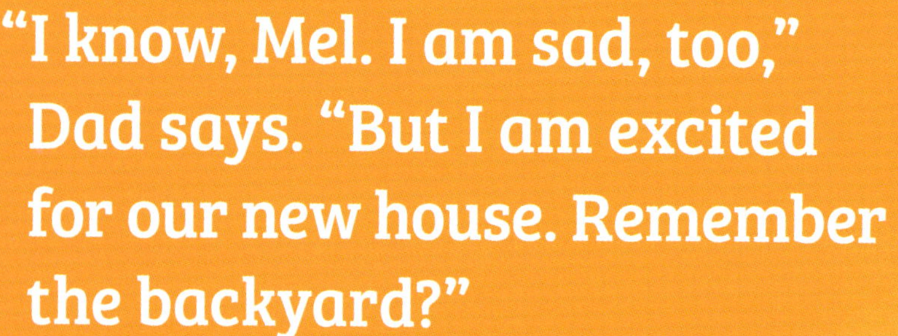

"I know, Mel. I am sad, too," Dad says. "But I am excited for our new house. Remember the backyard?"

"It was nice and big," I say.

I help Dad pack.

I am bringing my favorite things.

I feel a little better.

TOYS

I will miss my friends.
“We will visit you soon!” they say.

We wave goodbye to the house.

We get to our new house.

I pick out my room.

I can't wait for my friends to come over.

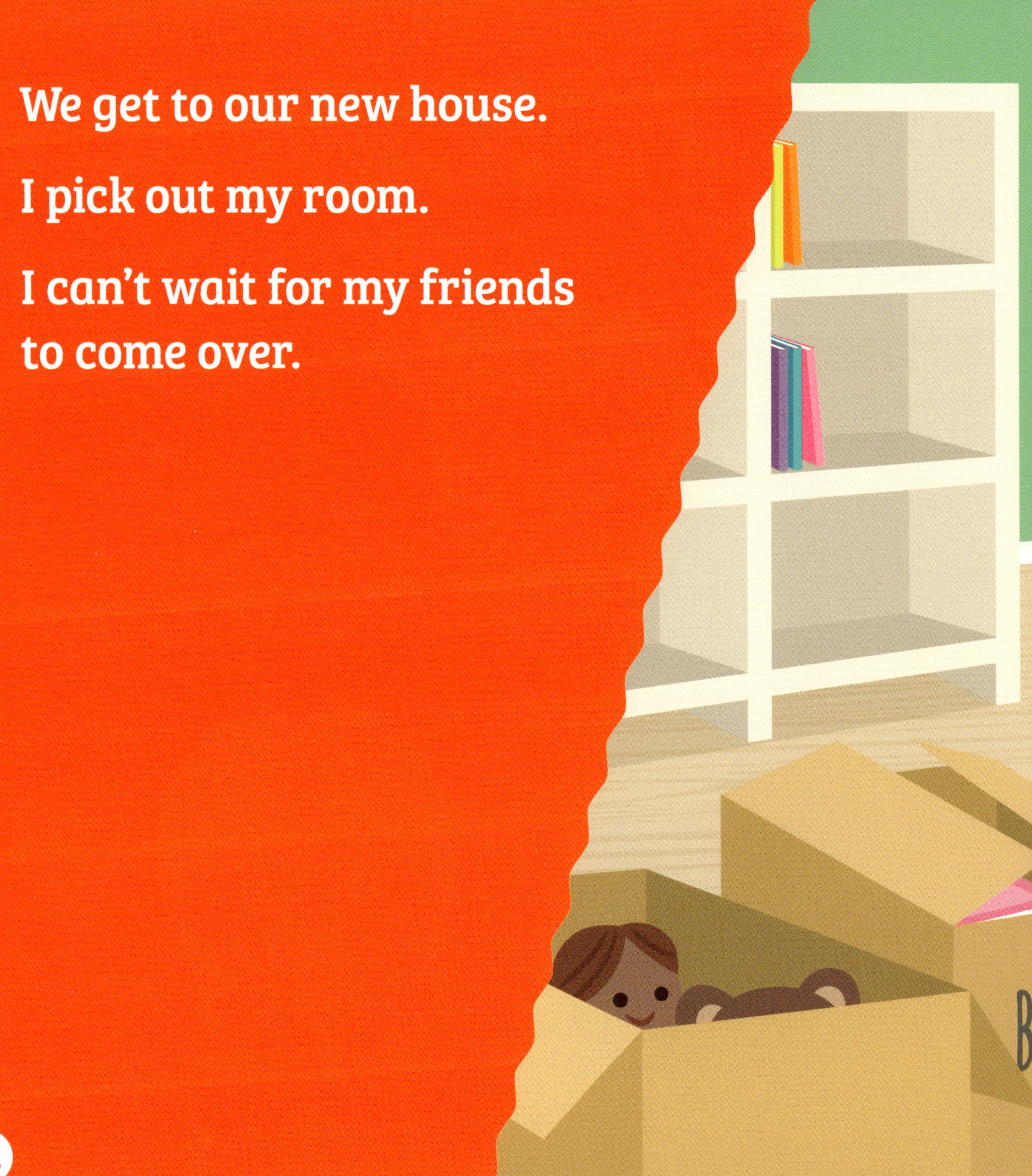

TOYS

I see kids in my new neighborhood.

Maybe we can be friends!

“Can I play?” I ask.

Let's Review!

What helps Mel feel better about moving to a new house?

A. Knowing her friends will visit soon.
B. Remembering her new backyard.
C. Refusing to pack.
D. Packing her favorite things.

Picture Glossary

backyard
An open area behind a home.

favorite
The things you like more than all the others.

neighborhood
An area where people live.

pack
To put things into a box or container to move them.

Let's Review! Answer Key: **A.** Knowing her friends will visit soon. **B.** Remembering her new backyard. **D.** Packing her favorite things.